To Iowa in the Back Seat

by Kristi R. Bradbury
illustrated by Joey Sotelo

To Robera, 6/14/22
Happy Birthday and happy reading! Kristi R. Bradbury

Copyright © 2021 by Kristi R. Bradbury

All rights reserved, including the right to reproduce this book, or portions thereof, in any form. No part of this book may be used or reproduced in any manner whatsoever without written permission from the publisher, except in the case of brief quotations embodied in critical articles and reviews. The views expressed herein are the responsibility of the author and do not necessarily represent the position of the publisher. For information or permission, visit **kristirbradbury.com**.

Published by In the Back Seat Books

Cover art by Joey Sotelo
Cover design by Steven Novak
Dedication page art by Angela Bradbury
Interior print design and layout by Marny K. Parkin
Ebook design and layout by Marny K. Parkin
Kristi Bradbury bio photo by Angela Bradbury
Joey Sotelo bio photo by Andrew Boone

Paperback 978-1-7370291-0-6
Hardcover 978-1-7370291-1-3

For my mama, Alice,
who traveled next to me in the back seat
and cheers for me always.

Tagging along with Kay on this trip is a curious cricket!
Find him hiding on almost every page, sometimes with a few of his friends.

Shivering and yawning, I plop into the back seat of the car for the long trip to Iowa. The sun just starts to shine on the dark, purple Colorado Rocky Mountains.

We drive and drive, and soon the golden prairie of Nebraska is all around us. Daddy drives first, with Mama sitting in the middle of the back seat so Michael and I won't fuss at each other. Sue always gets to sit up front because she is the biggest.
It isn't fair.

Daddy calls from a phone booth outside the car, and a lady on roller skates brings our food.

There is no leaving the car unless you really, really have to go because Grandma is expecting us for supper. We eat FAST. Gulping that cold, fizzy root beer is so yummy!

Now Mama drives, and Daddy naps in the back seat with his feet on Michael's lap and his head on mine.

And Daddy snores so loudly! Really not fair. So I lean my head out the window. I love the warm breeze on my face and the sound of swishing grasses, but Daddy's heavy head makes my legs tingly. Good thing he wakes up and drives again.

Up ahead is the mile-wide Missouri River between Nebraska and Iowa. While we cross the bridge, we sing "Over the River and Through the Woods, to Grandmother's House We Go." ALL the verses.

Michael and I count the cows on all the hills and farms until one of us first spots the water tower in Grandma's town, high above the evening skyline. From the back seat we both scream, "I see the water tower! I win!" Then we fuss. Daddy proclaims Sue the winner because of our fussing. NOT FAIR.

After kisses and MORE kisses from Grandma, I run inside to the candy dish. Rattle, rattle, rattle goes the lid as I bounce across the creaky floor. Mmm! Peppermint ribbon candy.

The smell of Grandma's fried chicken makes my tummy rumble.

The grownups talk and talk during supper, so I listen to crickets outside the open window. That's my favorite Iowa sound.

The next day, Grandpa walks us to his restaurant, the Uptown Café.

I spin around on a tall stool at the counter, and Grandpa makes me a vanilla sundae with chocolate sauce and a cherry on top. He laughs at my chocolate mustache, and I giggle, too, because he laughs like a horse!

Grandma's attic is the best. Michael and I go on adventures up there every day. We battle pirates and sharks and hunt for buried treasure.

That's when I see it—
a dusty wooden game board.

I run downstairs and holler, "Grandma, what is this?"

"Kay, you found my favorite Chinese checkers game from when I was your age," Grandma says with a smile.

"I'll teach you to play." We play all week. She says I'm really good, but I think she lets me win.

Grandma holds a Chinese checkers marble. "Take this with you," she says. "It'll remind you of me."

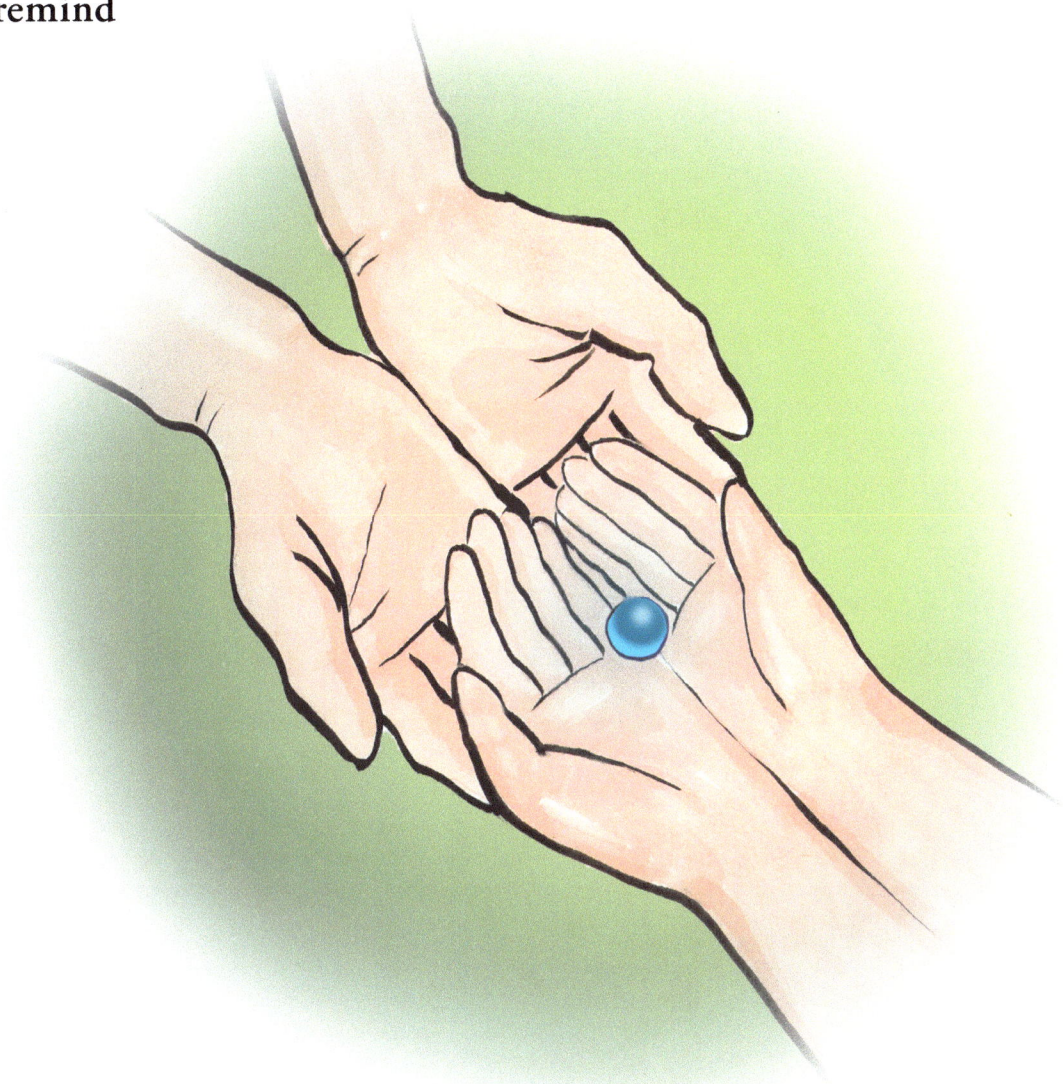

I put it in my pocket.

But then I feel the marble!
I pull it from my pocket
and remember Grandma.
That helps the prairie
feel less boring and the
back seat less unfair.

We are home.

Soon I'll drift to sleep
and dream about my next trip—
even if I'm in the back seat.

How many of you know the song, "Over the River and Through the Woods"? Kay's family sang it every time they drove over the river into Iowa. Even if you know the song, you probably don't know its history. This song came from a poem by Lydia Maria Child that was first published as "The New-England Boy's Song about Thanksgiving Day" in *Flowers for Children,* Volume 2.

Lydia Maria Child (February 11, 1802–October 20, 1880) was a novelist, journalist, teacher, poet, and rights activist. Originally, this poem had twelve stanzas, but only three or four are typically included in the song we know and love today. Eventually, her poem was set to music, but the composer of the tune is unknown.

(Source: "The Story Behind Over the River and Through the Woods," The Tabernacle Choir Blog, November 21, 2018, www.thetabernaclechoir.org/articles/over-the-river-and-through-the-wood.html.)

Kristi R. Bradbury

Kristi R. (Rohdy) Bradbury grew up enjoying road trips across the USA with her family. She shared stories of her adventures with her children, and, for a decade, she talked about writing them into books. The pandemic of 2020, with the need to stay at home, finally provided her the opportunity! Publishing this book is an accomplishment that fills her with a joy she hopes will be imparted to readers of all ages. Kristi has worked in special education for twenty years. She is the proud mom of five children and grandma of nine. She and her husband, Bill, live in Los Angeles.

Acknowledgments

Thank you Bill, A & J, D & B, B & C, D & T, Angela, and all my grandkids for your ideas! Thank you to the real Michael, Sue, Daddy, and Mama, and for all my cousins who gave me my childhood memories. Thank you LHS for always cheering. *KRB*

Joey Sotelo

Joey Sotelo is a graphic design student at Santa Monica College. He's been drawing since childhood, inspired by his enjoyment of endless illustrated library books. He lives in Los Angeles.

Acknowledgments

Thank you to my mom for her continual feedback on my work. Thank you to the professors who shared with me their treasury of knowledge. The biggest thanks goes to Kristi R. Bradbury for helping me kick-start my career. *JS*

Did you find me?

CPSIA information can be obtained
at www.ICGtesting.com
Printed in the USA
BVHW091940260921
617469BV00001B/7